Gelato

DRI DRI Gelato

Simple recipes for authentic Italian gelato to make at home

Adriano di Petrillo

Photography by Steve Painter

RYLAND
PETERS
& SMALL

LONDON NEW YORK

Design, Photography and Prop Styling
Steve Painter
Editor Rebecca Woods
Production Gary Hayes
Art Director Leslie Harrington
Editorial Director Julia Charles

Food Stylist Lucy Mckelvie
Indexer Hilary Bird

First published in 2012 by
Ryland Peters & Small
20–21 Jockey's Fields
London WC1R 4BW
and
519 Broadway, 5th Floor
New York, NY 10012
www.rylandpeters.com

10 9 8 7 6 5 4 3 2 1

Text and illustrations © AdiP Gelato Ltd 2012
Design and photographs
© Ryland Peters & Small 2012

Printed in China

UK ISBN: 978 1 84975 208 4
US ISBN: 978 1 84975 249 7

A CIP record for this book is available from the British Library.

US Library of Congress cataloging-in-publication data has been
applied for.

Notes

• All spoon measurements are level, unless otherwise specified.

• Uncooked or partially cooked eggs should not be served to the very
young, the very old, those with compromised immune systems, or to
pregnant women.

• When a recipe calls for the grated or pared peel of citrus fruit, buy
unwaxed fruit and wash well before using. If you can only find treated
fruit, scrub well in warm soapy water and rinse before using.

• All weights given for fruit are prepared weight.

• The gelato, sorbetto and granita shown in the photographs in this book
were all made using two different models of domestic ice cream maker –
the Gaggia Gelateria Ice Cream Maker and the Cuisinart Professional Ice
Cream Maker. For best results we strongly recommend that you use an
electric ice cream maker. However, if a machine is not available, you can
still try the following by-hand method, although the resulting product will
not be as light in texture. Simply pour your prepared gelato, sorbetto or
granita mixture into a lidded freezer-proof box and place in the freezer.
Remove the box every hour or so, transfer the contents to a large mixing
bowl and whisk with an electric hand mixer to break up any larger ice
crystals. Return the mixture to the box and then to the freezer. Repeat this
process every hour until the gelato, sorbetto or granita is frozen.

Contents

Dri Dri local Italian gelato

In Italy, gelato is a fundamental part of our diet from a very early age. When I was young, I was particularly keen on gelato and particularly lucky to live across the street from the best gelateria in Parma, my home town.

Everyday after school I would stop at the gelateria and have my cone with crema gelato and lemon sorbet (definitely a very strange combination, but I loved it), while my mother was buying a large tub to take home and serve for dessert. The problem was that most of the time I managed to sneak into the kitchen and finish the whole tub by myself before dinner had even started!

The owner of the gelateria was Daniele, a gentleman with an incredible passion for this magical product and top notch recipes. One afternoon he showed me how the gelato was being made and let me assist him in preparing a lemon sorbet. I remember running back home with a tub of the gelato I had made myself, feeling very proud and accomplished at the age of five.

My life went on and I began to travel a lot for study and work, living in Milan, Boston, New York and finally settling in London. Throughout, one constant in my life

was my passion for gelato, but unfortunately I was never able to find a gelateria that could match the unbelievable gelato of my friend Daniele.

During those years, I realized that gelato holds a special place in people's hearts. Anyone who has been to Italy will tell you that gelato is one of the key memories of their vacation. There is something very romantic and sentimental about gelato and people relate to it in a special way. I recognized the opportunity I had to bring the gelato experience I had as a child to the rest of the world. I went back to Parma and told Daniele I wanted to introduce his gelato around the world, starting in London. That is the moment when Dri Dri was born.

I worked for months to develop recipes that would combine the artisanal Italian tradition with a modern cosmopolitan product that is entirely natural. I travelled extensively to source specific ingredients that would make Dri Dri gelato even more special and worked with Daniele to simplify his recipes and eliminate all kinds of additives that are typically used in gelato making. The result is an amazingly tasty and creamy product that is very pure and light, low in fat and easy to digest.

We have a very strict philosophy at Dri Dri: our gelato must be made with the best ingredients that we select from all over the world: we use Gran Cru chocolate from São Tomé to make the Extra Dark Chocolate Sorbet, our pistachios are imported from Sicily and we use only Tonda Gentile hazelnuts from Piedmont. High quality ingredients mean there is no need for artificial flavourings, colourings, emulsifiers, preservatives or non-natural thickeners. Because we do not use any additives we have to keep the gelato in closed containers (called *pozzetti*) that allow a very strict temperature control. Be mindful: every time you enter a gelateria where you can see the gelato, it means they are using additives, otherwise it would melt.

We opened our first store in 2010 on the iconic Portobello Road in London, where people from all over the world pass by. We decorated the interior in natural materials such as marble and wood to show our commitment to using natural ingredients in the gelato and created a bold logo which was simple, colourful and friendly. The second store opened in Chelsea Farmers Market in 2011, and is quickly becoming a destination for all west Londoners, especially when the sun is shining! We will open other stores as the word about Dri Dri spreads.

Enjoying gelato, sorbetto and granita at home

I am pleased to see the rise in popularity of gelato and sorbetto outside of Italy. For me it is such an integral part of my childhood and this is one of the reasons we now teach children how to make gelato in our stores. Every day we run classes for children where they can draw their own labels, watch the gelato being churned and scoop it into cones. But not everyone is within walking distance of a Dri Dri and so this book is aimed at teaching you the secrets of Dri Dri so you can make delicious gelato at home.

All you need to make delcious fresh gelato, sorbetto and granita at home is a gelato or ice-cream maker. The key to the creamy texture of gelato is the combined action of churning as it freezes using a method called 'mantecazione'. The continued stirring of the liquid means that air isn't absorbed and the gelato is silky smooth. The best results come from gelato or ice-cream machines that have a built-in compressor – the machines that have a canister which you pre-freeze do not result in as light a product, so if you are serious about your gelato, it may be worth investing that little bit more for the perfect result.

Apart from the gelato maker, you don't need any specialist equipment, although a food processor is very useful for puréeing fruit for sorbets, especially tougher fruits, such as pineapple. Softer fruits, such as berries and mango, can be puréed easily with a hand blender. For a smoother finish, you may also like to pass the puréed fruit through a sieve/strainer before adding it to the gelato-maker to get rid of the seeds, but this is not essential.

Gelato starts with a dairy base, but unlike traditional ice cream, gelato is made using more milk than cream, which gives it a lighter texture. You should be able to eat a whole tub of gelato and never feel full! Flavourings are added to the base, along with a little egg white, which acts as a natural binder and also thickens the gelato. The quantities of the base ingredients may fluctuate depending on the added ingredients, so that each gelato is perfectly balanced in flavour and texture. As the taste of the gelato depends very much on the ingredients used, we always insist on using organic cream, milk and sugar and only ever free-range eggs.

Preparing sorbetto and granita is also very simple to do at home. They, too, start with a simple base, this time of syrup, to which flavourings are added – usually fresh fruits but other flavours, such as coffee, are also popular. Granita is different from sorbetto in two ways: firstly it is not as sweet as sorbet, containing much more water than syrup, and, secondly, it has a much coarser texture.

For the flavourings, we ship our ingredients in from around the world to ensure that we only serve the best, but as long as you look for the highest quality you can buy in the supermarket, you can't go too far wrong. Perhaps the exception to this is fresh fruits, which are never better than when they are locally grown and picked at the peak of ripeness. Only ever use what is in season where you are as air-freighting fruit over long distances stops natural ripening and impairs flavour. Around the festive season, when fruit is less abundant, richer flavours of gelato such as Chocolate, Tiramisú, Bacio and Salted Caramel are a perfect indulgence, while in summer you can take your pick of gelato or sorbetto and granita prepared with ripe summer berries and zingy citrus fruits.

Gelato and sorbetto is always best served fresh out of the machine as it is at the perfect texture and the fresh ingredients still have all their flavour. As preservatives aren't used, natural flavourings do begin to lose their intensity, and although they will keep in a domestic freezer for a few days, the quality is never as good as when freshly made. And with most gelato machines able to whip up a batch in about 25 minutes, there is no excuse for not preparing it freshly every time.

As well as recipes for gelato, sorbetto and granita, the last chapter suggests other ways you can enjoy them, such as sweet treats to pair them with and twists for refreshing sorbetto and gelato-based drinks. To finish we have added a chart of some of the most popular flavour pairings created in our stores, so you are never short of inspiration!

Gelato

madagascan vanilla gelato
gelato alla vaniglia del madagascar

Madagascan vanilla is perhaps the finest in the world. Harvesting the pods is incredbily labour-intensive, making it a luxury item. This lavish gelato uses four pods but is one of the best ways to appreciate the pure, rich flavour of vanilla. Serve on it's own or it is the perfect accompaniment for fresh fruit.

500 ml/2 cups organic whole milk

165 ml/⅔ cup organic whipping cream

4 Madagascan vanilla pods/beans

160 g/¾ cup plus 1 tablespoon organic (caster) sugar

1 free-range egg white

Serves 4

Put the milk and whipping cream in a small saucepan and heat gently until it reaches boiling point.

Use a sharp knife to split the vanilla pod lengthways and scrape the seeds from the pods into the milk mixture. Stir, then pour the mixture into a heat-resistant bowl and refrigerate for 20 minutes.

In a large mixing bowl and using an electric hand whisk, beat together the sugar and egg white until it forms soft peaks when the beaters are lifted out of the mixture. Add the chilled milk mixture and whisk for a further 20 seconds.

Pour the mixture into the gelato maker and churn freeze according to the manufacturer's instructions.

The gelato is best served immediately or can be kept in the freezer for up to 3–4 days.

yogurt gelato
gelato allo yogurt

With all the frenzy about fat-free yogurt, we want to propose a recipe based on a traditional whole yogurt: the creamier the better! Yogurt gelato is perfect served with one of the berry sorbets, or try topping it with honey and toasted almonds or simply with fresh organic fruit.

500 ml/2 cups organic whole milk

50 ml/¼ cup organic whipping cream

1 vanilla pod/bean, split lengthways

160 g/¾ cup plus 1 tablespoon organic (caster) sugar

1 free-range egg white

250 g/1 cup organic whole yogurt

ripe organic raspberries, to serve (optional)

Serves 4

Put the milk and whipping cream in a small saucepan and heat gently until it reaches boiling point. Pour the mixture into a heat-resistant bowl, add the vanilla pod and stir. Refrigerate for 20 minutes.

In a large mixing bowl and using an electric hand whisk, beat together the sugar and egg white until it forms soft peaks when the beaters are lifted out of the mixture. Stir in the yogurt.

Remove the chilled milk mixture from the refrigerator and discard the vanilla pod. Pour into the sugar and egg mixture and whisk for a further 20 seconds.

Pour the mixture into the gelato maker and churn freeze according to the manufacturer's instructions.

The gelato is best served immediately or can be kept in the freezer for up to 3–4 days.

salted butter gelato
gelato al burro salato

The Breton butter that we use to flavour Dri Dri's Salted Butter Gelato is notable for it's high salt content, which is in coarse grains visible in the butter and adds an interesting contrast to the creamy nature of the gelato.

600 ml/2½ cups organic whole milk

65 ml/⅓ cup organic whipping cream

60 g/5 tablespoons salted butter, such as Breton butter

1 vanilla pod/bean, split lengthways

160 g/¾ cup plus 1 tablespoon organic (caster) sugar

1 free-range egg white

Serves 4

Put the milk and whipping cream in a small saucepan and heat gently until it reaches boiling point. Add the butter and stir until it has melted and the mixture is smooth. Pour the mixture into a heat-resistant bowl, add the vanilla pod and stir. Refrigerate for 20 minutes.

In a mixing bowl and using an electric hand whisk, beat together the sugar and egg white until it forms soft peaks when the beaters are lifted out of the bowl.

Remove the chilled milk mixture from the refrigerator and discard the vanilla pod. Pour into the sugar and egg mixture and whisk for a further 20 seconds.

Pour the mixture into the gelato maker and churn freeze according to the manufacturer's instructions. The gelato is best served immediately or can be kept in the freezer for up to 3–4 days.

chocolate gelato
gelato al cioccolato

For our classic chocolate gelato we source the finest quality chocolate from Dutch traders, but you can just go to your local supermarket and buy the best quality available!

500 ml/2 cups organic whole milk

165 ml/⅔ cup organic whipping cream

20 g/¾ oz. dark chocolate (70% cocoa solids)

160 g/¾ cup plus 1 tablespoon organic (caster) sugar

1 free-range egg white

80 g/⅔ cup unsweetened cocoa powder

small waffle cones, to serve (optional)

Serves 4

Put the milk and whipping cream in a small saucepan and heat gently until it reaches boiling point. Pour the mixture into a heat-resistant bowl and refrigerate for 20 minutes.

Melt the dark chocolate in a heat-resistant bowl set over a pan of barely simmering water, making sure the base of the bowl does not touch the water.

In a large mixing bowl and using an electric hand whisk, beat together the sugar, egg white, cocoa powder and melted dark chocolate until it forms soft peaks when the beaters are lifted out of the mixture. Add the chilled milk mixture and whisk for a further 20 seconds.

Pour the mixture into the gelato maker and churn freeze according to the manufacturer's instructions.

The gelato is best served immediately or can be kept in the freezer for up to 3–4 days.

mint chocolate chip gelato
gelato alla stracciatella di menta

Mint and chocolate is a perfect pairing. We use peppermint grown in Pancalieri in the Piedmont region of Italy, which is world renowned for its mint and other herbs.

500 ml/2 cups organic whole milk

165 ml/⅔ cup organic whipping cream

1 vanilla pod/bean, split lengthways

160 g/¾ cup plus 1 tablespoon organic (caster) sugar

1 free-range egg white

50 g/2 handfuls fresh mint leaves, finely chopped

100 g/3½ oz. dark chocolate (70% cocoa solids), finely chopped

Serves 4

Put the milk and whipping cream in a small saucepan and heat gently until it reaches boiling point. Pour the mixture into a heat-resistant bowl, add the vanilla pod and stir. Refrigerate for 20 minutes.

In a large mixing bowl and using an electric hand whisk, beat together the sugar and egg white until it forms soft peaks when the beaters are lifted out of the mixture.

Remove the chilled milk mixture from the refrigerator and discard the vanilla pod. Pour into the sugar and egg mixture and whisk for a further 20 seconds. Stir in the chopped mint and let it rest for 30 minutes.

Pour the mixture into the gelato maker and churn freeze according to the manufacturer's instructions. About 5 minutes before the end of the process, add the chocolate chips into the mixture in the gelato maker, and continue churning so they are mixed through.

The gelato is best served immediately or can be kept in the freezer for up to 3–4 days.

chocolate chip gelato
gelato alla stracciatella

The classic method for stracciatella gelato is to pour the hot melted chocolate directly into the gelato as it churns, which solidifies the chocolate and distributes it throughout the gelato. In this method, the chocolate is chopped rather than poured, which means more generous bites of chocolate, but you can make it in whichever method you wish.

500 ml/2 cups organic whole milk

165 ml/⅔ cup organic whipping cream

1 vanilla pod/bean, split lengthways

160 g/¾ cup plus 1 tablespoon organic (caster) sugar

1 free-range egg white

100 g/3½ oz. dark chocolate (70% cocoa solids), finely chopped

Serves 4

Put the milk and whipping cream in a small saucepan and heat gently until it reaches boiling point. Pour the mixture into a heat-resistant bowl, add the vanilla pod and stir. Refrigerate for 20 minutes.

In a large mixing bowl and using an electric hand whisk, beat together the sugar and egg white until it forms soft peaks when the beaters are lifted out of the mixture.

Remove the chilled milk mixture from the refrigerator and discard the vanilla pod. Pour into the sugar and egg mixture and whisk for a further 20 seconds.

Pour the mixture into the gelato maker and churn freeze according to the manufacturer's instructions. About 5 minutes before the end of the process, add the chocolate chips into the mixture in the gelato maker, and continue churning so they are mixed through.

The gelato is best served immediately or can be kept in the freezer for up to 3–4 days.

extra dark chocolate gelato
gelato al cioccolato extra noir

The chocolate we use for our Extra Dark Chocolate Gelato is from the island republic of São Tomé. The cocoa grown there is bitter and smoky and rich in flavour. If you can find this locally or online, it's perfect for this sophisticated gelato, but any good single origin chocolate can be used.

500 ml/2 cups organic whole milk

165 ml/⅔ cup organic whipping cream

80 g/2½ oz. dark chocolate (70% cocoa solids), finely chopped

160 g/¾ cup plus 1 tablespoon organic (caster) sugar

1 free-range egg white

200 g/1½ cups unsweetened cocoa powder

Serves 4

Put the milk and whipping cream in a small saucepan and heat gently until it reaches boiling point. Pour the mixture into a heat-resistant bowl and refrigerate for 20 minutes.

Melt the dark chocolate in a heat-resistant bowl set over a pan of barely simmering water, making sure the base of the bowl does not touch the water.

In a large mixing bowl and using an electric hand whisk, beat together the sugar, egg white, cocoa powder and melted dark chocolate until it forms soft peaks when the beaters are lifted out of the mixture. Add the chilled milk mixture and whisk for a further 20 seconds until well combined.

Pour the mixture into the gelato maker and churn freeze according to the manufacturer's instructions.

The gelato is best served immediately or can be kept in the freezer for up to 3–4 days.

espresso coffee gelato
gelato al caffé espresso

Sumatran coffee beans are some of the most sought after in the world. Their smooth yet complex flavour brings rich depth to this gelato. If you can't find Sumatran, simply look for a coffee that is composed from 100% arabica beans.

500 ml/2 cups organic whole milk

165 ml/⅔ cup organic whipping cream

160 g/¾ cup plus 1 tablespoon organic (caster) sugar

1 free-range egg white

150 ml/⅔ cup espresso made with organic 100% arabica Sumatra Lington coffee beans, cooled

Serves 4

Put the milk and cream in a small saucepan and heat gently until it reaches boiling point. Pour the mixture into a heat-resistant bowl and refrigerate for 20 minutes.

In a large mixing bowl and using an electric hand whisk, beat together the sugar and egg white until it forms soft peaks when the beaters are lifted out of the mixture. Stir in the cooled coffee then add the chilled milk mixture and whisk for a further 20 seconds.

Pour the mixture into the gelato maker and churn freeze according to the manufacturer's instructions.

The gelato is best served immediately or can be kept in the freezer for up to 3–4 days.

cinnamon gelato
gelato alla cannella

There's something about adding a warm spice to cool gelato that makes this an irresistible variation. Cinnamon has been a prized luxury since ancient times, a spice fit for a king. We like to think the same about our gelato.

500 ml/2 cups organic whole milk

165 ml/⅔ cup organic whipping cream

1 vanilla pod/bean, split lengthways

160 g/¾ cup plus 1 tablespoon organic (caster) sugar

1 free-range egg white

50 g/3 tablespoons ground cinnamon, plus extra to dust

Serves 4

Put the milk and whipping cream in a small saucepan and heat gently until it reaches boiling point. Pour the mixture into a heat-resistant bowl, add the vanilla pod and stir. Refrigerate for 20 minutes.

In a large mixing bowl and using an electric hand whisk, beat together the sugar and egg white until it forms soft peaks when the beaters are lifted out of the mixture. Stir in the ground cinnamon.

Remove the chilled milk mixture from the refrigerator and discard the vanilla pod. Pour into the sugar and egg mixture and whisk for a further 20 seconds.

Pour the mixture into the gelato maker and churn freeze according to the manufacturer's instructions.

The gelato is best served immediately or can be kept in the freezer for up to 3–4 days. Serve dusted with extra cinnamon.

cookies and cream gelato
gelato al biscotto

Every nation has its own biscotto! At Dri Dri we use artisan cookies from a small town in Emilia Romagna called Lugo. If you do not find yourself regularly in Lugo, Speculoos cookies – available at most supermarkets – will work just fine!

500 ml/2 cups organic whole milk

165 ml/⅔ cup organic whipping cream

110 g/4 oz. Speculoos/Dutch Windmill cookies (about 4 cookies), plus extra to serve

160 g/¾ cup plus 1 tablespoon organic (caster) sugar

1 free-range egg white

Serves 4

Put the milk and cream in a small saucepan and heat gently until it reaches boiling point. Pour the mixture into a heat-resistant bowl and refrigerate for 20 minutes.

Blitz the cookies to a fine crumb in a food processor.

In a large mixing bowl and using an electric hand whisk, beat together the sugar and egg white until it forms soft peaks when the beaters are lifted out of the mixture. Stir in the cookie crumbs.

Remove the chilled milk mixture from the refrigerator, pour into the sugar and egg mixture and whisk for a further 20 seconds.

Pour the mixture into the gelato maker and churn freeze according to the manufacturer's instructions.

The gelato is best served immediately or can be kept in the freezer for up to 3–4 days. Serve sprinkled with extra crushed cookies.

hazelnut gelato
gelato alla nocciola

The Tonda Gentile hazelnut is grown in the Piedmont region of Italy, and is prized by chefs for its high quality, so it is naturally Dri Dri's first choice, too.

500 ml/2 cups organic whole milk

165 ml/⅔ cup organic whipping cream

140 g/1 cup shelled Tonda Gentile Trilobata hazelnuts, skins removed, plus extra to serve

½ teaspoon sea salt

160 g/¾ cup plus 1 tablespoon organic (caster) sugar

1 free-range egg white

Serves 4

Put the milk and cream in a small saucepan and heat gently until it reaches the boiling point. Pour the mixture into a heat-resistant bowl and refrigerate for 20 minutes.

In a dry frying pan, lightly toast the hazelnuts with the salt and set aside to cool. When cooled, grind the hazelnuts to a paste in a food processor.

In a large mixing bowl and using an electric hand whisk, beat together the sugar and egg white until it forms soft peaks when the beaters are lifted out of the mixture. Stir in the hazelnut paste.

Remove the chilled milk mixture from the refrigerator and pour into the sugar and egg mixture and whisk for a further 20 seconds.

Pour the mixture into the gelato maker and churn freeze according to the manufacturer's instructions.

The gelato is best served immediately or can be kept in the freezer for up to 3–4 days. Serve sprinkled with extra chopped hazelnuts.

tiramisú gelato
gelato tiramisú

What could be better than real Italian gelato combined with another of Italy's most famous sweet exports? Tiramisú literally means 'lift me up' in Italian, which this delicious, creamy gelato is guaranteed to do!

600 ml/2 cups organic whole milk

150 ml/⅔ cup organic whipping cream

50 ml/3 tablespoons port wine

3 free-range egg yolks, plus 1 egg white

1 vanilla pod/bean, split lengthways

150 g/¾ cup organic (caster) sugar

200 ml/¾ cup prepared espresso coffee, chilled

5 Savoiardi (ladyfinger) cookies, broken into small pieces

chocolate curls, to garnish

Serves 4

Put the milk and cream in a small saucepan and heat gently until it reaches boiling point. Add the port wine and the egg yolks and whisk together. Add the vanilla pod, pour the mixture into a heat-resistant bowl and refrigerate for 20 minutes.

In a large mixing bowl and using an electric hand whisk, beat together the sugar and egg white until it forms soft peaks when the beaters are lifted out of the mixture. Add 150 ml/⅔ cup of the coffee and quickly whisk in.

Remove the chilled milk mixture from the refrigerator and discard the vanilla pod. Pour into the sugar and egg mixture and whisk for a further 20 seconds.

Pour the mixture into the gelato maker and churn freeze according to the manufacturer's instructions.

While the mixture is freezing, dip the Savoiardi cookies into the remaining coffee. About 5 minutes before the end of the process, add the soaked cookies into the mixture in the gelato maker, and continue churning so they are mixed through.

The gelato is best served immediately or can be kept in the freezer for up to 3–4 days. Serve garnished with chocolate curls.

white chocolate and toasted hazelnut gelato
gelato al cioccolato bianco e nocciole tostate

Indulgent white chocolate and toasted hazelnut gelato is perfect for winter, especially around the holidays. Try offering it as an alternative dessert at a Christmas lunch.

650 ml/2⅔ cups organic whole milk

150 ml/⅔ cup organic whipping cream

100 g/3½ oz. white chocolate, chopped

1 vanilla pod/bean, split lengthways

50 g/⅓ cup shelled hazelnuts, skins removed

½ teaspoon sea salt

150 g/¾ cup organic (caster) sugar

1 free-range egg white

Serves 4

Put the milk and cream in a small saucepan and heat gently until it reaches boiling point. Remove from the heat and add the white chocolate, stirring until it melts. Add the split vanilla pod, pour the mixture into a heat-resistant bowl and refrigerate for 20 minutes.

In a dry frying pan/skillet, lightly toast the hazelnuts with the salt and set aside to cool.

In a large mixing bowl and using an electric hand whisk, beat together the sugar and egg white until it forms soft peaks when the beaters are lifted out of the mixture.

Remove the chilled milk mixture from the refrigerator and discard the vanilla pod. Pour into the sugar and egg mixture and whisk for a further 20 seconds.

Pour the mixture into the gelato maker and churn freeze according to the manufacturer's instructions. About 5 minutes before the end of the process, add the toasted hazelnuts into the mixture in the gelato maker, and continue churning so they are mixed through.

The gelato is best served immediately or can be kept in the freezer for up to 3–4 days.

sicilian pistachio gelato
gelato al pistacchio siciliano

The pistachios used in Dri Dri's pistachio gelato come directly from Sicily, where they are grown in the volcanic soil of Mount Etna and have a distinctive long, thin shape and a sharp taste.

500 ml/2 cups organic whole milk

165 ml/⅔ cup organic whipping cream

140 g/1 cup shelled pistachio nuts, skins removed

½ teaspoon sea salt

165 g/¾ cup plus 1 tablespoon organic (caster) sugar

1 free-range organic egg white

For the pistachio brittle

25 g/1 oz. pistachio nuts, shelled

25 g/1 oz. organic (caster) sugar

a baking sheet lined with a piece of oiled kitchen foil

Serves 4

Put the milk and cream in a small saucepan and heat gently until it reaches boiling point. Pour the mixture into a heat-resistant bowl and refrigerate for 20 minutes.

In a dry frying pan/skillet, lightly toast the pistachios with the salt and set aside to cool. When cooled, grind the pistachios to a paste in a food processor.

In a large mixing bowl and using an electric hand whisk, beat together the sugar and egg white until it forms soft peaks when the beaters are lifted out of the mixture. Stir in the pistachio paste.

Remove the chilled milk mixture from the refrigerator, pour into the sugar and egg mixture and whisk for a further 20 seconds.

Pour the mixture into the gelato maker and churn freeze according to the manufacturer's instructions.

While the gelato is churning, make the pistachio brittle. Soak the pistachios in boiling water for 4–5 minutes to soften their skins, then peel and pat dry. Put the peeled nuts and the sugar into a frying pan/skillet and heat over a medium heat until the sugar has melted and is bubbling. Tip onto the prepared baking sheet and set aside until the sugar has cooled and set, then break into shards.

Serve the gelato in bowls garnished with shards of pistachio brittle.

The gelato is best served immediately but can be kept in the freezer for up to 3–4 days.

salted caramel gelato
gelato al caramello salato

We serve only the best at Dri Dri! Our gourmet Salted Caramel Gelato is salted with Himalayan pink crystal salt, thought to be the purest salt there is, formed in ancient unpolluted seas. It brings out the taste of the caramel perfectly.

500 ml/2 cups organic whole milk

160 ml/⅔ cup organic whipping cream

1 vanilla pod/bean, split lengthways

80 ml/⅓ cup spring water

½ teaspoon Himalayan pink salt

210 g/1 cup plus 1 tablespoon organic (caster) sugar

1 free-range egg white

For the caramel shards

100 g/½ cup organic (caster) sugar

a baking sheet lined with a piece of oiled kitchen foil

Serves 4

Put the milk and cream in a small saucepan and heat gently until it reaches boiling point. Pour the mixture into a heat-resistant bowl, add the vanilla pod and stir. Refrigerate for 20 minutes.

To prepare the salted caramel, put the spring water, salt and 80 g/7 tablespoons of the sugar in a small saucepan and heat gently, stirring, until it reaches boiling point, thickens and turns a golden colour. Remove from the heat immediately and let cool.

In a large mixing bowl and using an electric hand whisk, beat together the remaining sugar and the egg white until it forms soft peaks when the beaters are lifted out of the mixture. Stir in the cooled salted caramel.

Remove the chilled milk mixture from the refrigerator and discard the vanilla pod. Pour into the sugar and egg mixture and whisk for a further 20 seconds.

Pour the mixture into the gelato maker and churn freeze according to the manufacturer's instructions.

While the gelato is churning, make the caramel shards. Sprinkle the sugar lightly over the prepared baking sheet. Put the baking sheet under a preheated grill/broiler and cook until the sugar melts and turns to caramel. Set aside until the caramel has cooled and set, then break into shards.

Serve the gelato in bowls garnished with shards of caramel.

The gelato is best served immediately but can be kept in the freezer for up to 3–4 days.

licorice gelato
gelato alla liquirizia

Calabria is famous for its licorice, which grows naturally on the hillsides and has been harvested for hundreds of years. Calabrian licorice powder is available from many Italian delicatessens or specialist online shops.

500 ml/2 cups organic whole milk

165 ml/⅔ cup organic whipping cream

1 vanilla pod/bean, split lengthways

165 g/¾ cup plus 1 tablespoon organic (caster) sugar

1 free-range egg white

25 g/1 oz. powdered licorice

Serves 4

Put the milk and cream in a small saucepan and heat gently until it reaches boiling point. Pour the mixture into a heat-resistant bowl, add the vanilla pod and stir. Refrigerate for 20 minutes.

In a mixing bowl and using an electric hand whisk, beat together the sugar and egg white until it forms soft peaks when the beaters are lifted out of the mixture. Stir in the licorice powder.

Remove the chilled milk mixture from the refrigerator and discard the vanilla pod. Pour into the sugar and egg mixture and whisk for a further 20 seconds.

Pour the mixture into the gelato maker and churn freeze according to the manufacturer's instructions.

The gelato is best served immediately or can be kept in the freezer for up to 3–4 days.

malaga gelato
gelato malaga

Malaga gelato is the Italian version of rum and raisin, using Passito di Pantelleria wine – a wine made from grapes dried on straw mats.

50 g/⅓ cup raisins

50 ml/3 tablespoons straw wine, such as Passito di Pantelleria

700 ml/3 cups organic whole milk

150 ml/⅔ cup organic whipping cream

1 vanilla pod/bean, split lengthways

165 g/¾ cup plus 1 tablespoon organic (caster) sugar

1 free-range egg white

Serves 4

Put the raisins in a bowl and pour over the wine. Set aside to soak for 20 minutes.

Put the milk and whipping cream in a small saucepan and heat gently until it reaches boiling point. Add the wine-soaked raisins (including any soaking wine) and the vanilla pod and stir through. Pour the mixture into a heat-resistant bowl and refrigerate for 20 minutes.

In a mixing bowl and using an electric hand whisk, beat together the sugar and egg white until it forms soft peaks when the beaters are lifted out of the mixture.

Remove the chilled milk mixture from the refrigerator and discard the vanilla pod. Pour into the sugar and egg mixture and whisk for a further 20 seconds.

Pour the mixture into the gelato maker and churn freeze according to the manufacturer's instructions.

The gelato is best served immediately or can be kept in the freezer for up to 3–4 days.

dulce de leche gelato
gelato al dulce de leche

Dulce de leche is a caramel made from slowly cooking sweetened milk so that the sugar caramelizes. You can make it yourself, or it is widely available in jars.

600 ml/2½ cups organic whole milk

155 ml/⅔ cup organic whipping cream

90 g/6 tablespoons dulce de leche, plus extra to serve

1 vanilla pod/bean, split lengthways

130 g/⅔ cup organic (caster) sugar

1 free-range egg white

Serves 4

Put the milk and cream in a small saucepan and heat gently until it reaches boiling point. Add the dulce de leche and stir through until it melts. Add the split vanilla pod, pour the mixture into a heat-resistant bowl and refrigerate for 20 minutes.

In a mixing bowl and using an electric hand whisk, beat together the sugar and egg white until it forms soft peaks when the beaters are lifted out of the mixture.

Remove the chilled milk mixture from the refrigerator and discard the vanilla pod. Pour into the sugar and egg mixture and whisk for a further 20 seconds.

Pour the mixture into the gelato maker and churn freeze according to the manufacturer's instructions.

The gelato is best served immediately or can be kept in the freezer for up to 3–4 days. Serve drizzled with extra dulce de leche.

bacio gelato
gelato bacio

In Italy the combination of hazelnut and chocolate is often referred to as 'Bacio', after the famous candies by Perugina.

500 ml/2 cups organic whole milk

165 ml/⅔ cup organic whipping cream

80 g/½ cup shelled hazelnuts, skins removed

½ teaspoon salt

25 g/1 oz. dark chocolate (70% cocoa solids)

165 g/¾ cup plus 1 tablespoon organic (caster) sugar

1 free-range egg white

60 g/scant ½ cup unsweetened cocoa powder

Serves 4

Put the milk and cream in a small saucepan and heat gently until it reaches boiling point. Pour the mixture into a heat-resistant bowl and refrigerate for 20 minutes.

In a dry frying pan/skillet, lightly toast the hazelnuts with the salt and set aside to cool. When cooled, grind the hazelnuts to a paste in a food processor.

Melt the dark chocolate in a heat-resistant bowl set over a pan of barely simmering water.

In a large mixing bowl and using an electric hand whisk, beat together the sugar, egg white, cocoa powder and melted chocolate until it forms soft peaks when the beaters are lifted out of the mixture. Add the chilled milk mixture and whisk for a further 20 seconds.

Pour the mixture into the gelato maker and churn freeze according to the manufacturer's instructions.

The gelato is best served immediately or can be kept in the freezer for up to 3–4 days.

custard cream gelato with a hint of sorrento lemon

gelato alla crema aromatizzato al limone di sorrento

Crema is the most popular flavour in Italy. It is similar in taste to classic English egg custard, only frozen. At Dri Dri, we particularly love adding a touch of Sorrento lemon zest – it tones down the egg flavour and will pep you up!

1 lemon
500 ml/2 cups organic whole milk
165 ml/⅔ cup organic whipping cream
½ vanilla pod/bean, split lengthways
165 g/¾ cup plus 1 tablespoon organic (caster) sugar
3 free-range eggs

For the candied lemon peel

2 large lemons
50 g/¼ cup organic (golden caster) sugar

Serves 4

Use a sharp knife to pare slices of peel from half the lemon – you only need to use half the peel of the lemon but it is easier to do this if the lemon is whole.

Put the milk and cream in a small saucepan and heat gently until it reaches boiling point. Add the split vanilla pod and the lemon peel slices, pour the mixture into a heat-resistant bowl and refrigerate for 20 minutes.

In a mixing bowl and using an electric hand whisk, beat together the sugar and egg white until it forms soft peaks when the beaters are lifted out of the mixture.

Remove the chilled milk mixture from the refrigerator and use a slotted spoon to scoop out the lemon peel and vanilla pod and discard them. Pour into the sugar and egg mixture and whisk for a further 20 seconds.

Pour the mixture into the gelato maker and churn freeze according to the manufacturer's instructions.

While the gelato is churning, prepare the candied lemon peel. Pare the peel from the lemons in long curling strips, leaving behind any bitter white pith. Blanch the peel in a pan of boiling water for about 2 minutes, then drain.

Put the sugar and 100 ml/⅓ cup water in a small pan and heat until the sugar has dissolved. Bring to the boil, then boil for 1 minute. Add the lemon peel and simmer for 20 minutes, until it is opaque and the syrup is reduced. Lift the peel out with a fork and leave to dry on a wire rack set over some paper towels.

Serve the gelato in small bowls garnished with the candied peel.

The gelato is best served immediately but can be kept in the freezer for up to 3–4 days.

Sorbetto

strawberry sorbet
sorbetto alla fragola

The key to the sweetness and depth of flavour in this sorbet is the quality of strawberry used. You can't beat locally-grown organic strawberries, picked at perfect ripeness. Anything else will pale in comparison.

360 ml/1½ cups spring water

freshly squeezed juice of ½ lemon

160 g/¾ cup plus 1 tablespoon organic (caster) sugar

500 g/1 lb. 2 oz. ripe organic strawberries, hulled

Serves 4

In a saucepan set over medium heat, gently heat 160 ml/⅔ cup of the spring water until it reaches boiling point. Remove from the heat, add the lemon juice and stir in the sugar until it dissolves. Let the syrup cool for 30 minutes.

Put the strawberries and the remaining water into a food processor and blitz to a purée. Add the cooled syrup and blend briefly again until thoroughly mixed.

Pour the mixture into the gelato maker and churn freeze according to the manufacturer's instructions.

The sorbet is best served immediately or can be kept in the freezer for up to 3–4 days.

pineapple sorbet
sorbetto all'ananas

Pineapple sorbet is the perfect summer refresher – and great combined with coconut and mango flavoured sorbets. When you are trimming the pineapple, set aside some of its spiky leaves to use as a stunning garnish.

310 ml/1⅓ cups spring water

freshly squeezed juice of ½ lemon

160 g/¾ cup plus 1 tablespoon organic (caster) sugar

550 g/1 lb. 4 oz. ripe organic pineapple (about 1 pineapple), peel, cored and chopped

Serves 4

In a saucepan set over medium heat, gently heat 160 ml/⅔ cup of the spring water until it reaches boiling point. Remove from the heat, add the lemon juice and stir in the sugar until it dissolves. Let the syrup cool for 30 minutes.

Put the pineapple and remaining water into a food processor and blitz to a purée. Add the cooled syrup and blend briefly again until thoroughly mixed.

Pour the mixture into the gelato maker and churn freeze according to the manufacturer's instructions.

The sorbet is best served immediately or can be kept in the freezer for up to 3–4 days. Serve garnished with pineapple leaves, if desired.

banana sorbet
sorbetto alla banana

Bananas, with their smooth, soft texture, make the creamiest sorbets. Serve them paired with their classic partner – chocolate – by adding a scoop of Extra Dark Chocolate Gelato or just a drizzle of chocolate sauce.

360 ml/1½ cups spring water

freshly squeezed juice of ½ lemon

160 g/¾ cup plus 1 tablespoon organic (caster) sugar

500 g/1 lb. 2 oz. ripe organic bananas (about 5 bananas), peeled and chopped

Serves 4

In a saucepan set over medium heat, gently heat 160 ml/⅔ cup of the spring water until it reaches boiling point. Remove from the heat, add half the lemon juice and stir in the sugar until it dissolves. Let the syrup cool for 30 minutes.

Put the bananas and the remaining water in a food processor and blitz to a purée. Add the cooled syrup and the remaining lemon juice and blend briefly again until thoroughly mixed.

Pour the mixture into the gelato maker and churn freeze according to the manufacturer's instructions.

The sorbet is best served immediately or can be kept in the freezer for up to 3–4 days.

sorrento lemon sorbet
sorbetto al limone di sorrento

Sorrento is famous for its lemons, which are huge and weigh down the boughs of the trees on the roadside along the beautiful Amalfi coast. Reserve the husks and serve the lemon sorbet inside them in the traditional way.

610 ml/2½ cups spring water
200 ml/¾ cup freshly squeezed organic lemon juice (about 5 lemons), husks reserved
240 g/1 cup plus 3 tablespoons organic (caster) sugar

Serves 4

In a saucepan set over medium heat, gently heat 160 ml/⅔ cup of the spring water until it reaches boiling point. Remove from the heat, add 2 tablespoons of the lemon juice and stir in 160 g/¾ cup of the sugar until it dissolves. Let the syrup cool for 30 minutes.

Put the remaining lemon juice, water and sugar in a jug/pitcher and whisk together. Add the cooled syrup and whisk briefly again until thoroughly mixed.

Pour the mixture into the gelato maker and churn freeze according to the manufacturer's instructions.

Serve the sorbet spooned into the reserved lemon husks.

Sorbet is best served immediately but can be kept in the freezer for up to 3–4 days.

passion fruit sorbet
sorbetto al frutto della passione

Aromatic passion fruit makes one of the most wonderfully sweet sorbets. Leaving the seeds in creates a pretty speckled effect in the finished sorbet.

260 ml/generous 1 cup spring water
freshly squeezed juice of ½ lemon
160 g/¾ cup plus 1 tablespoon organic (caster) sugar
550 g/1 lb. 4 oz. ripe organic passion fruit pulp with seeds (about 18 passion fruits)

Serves 4

In a saucepan set over medium heat, gently heat 160 ml/⅔ cup of the spring water until it reaches boiling point. Remove from the heat, add the lemon juice and stir in the sugar until it dissolves. Let the syrup cool for 30 minutes.

Put the passion fruit pulp and seeds and the remaining water in a food processor and blitz until combined but the seeds are still quite whole. Add the cooled syrup and blend briefly again until thoroughly mixed. Pour the mixture into the gelato maker and churn freeze according to the manufacturer's instructions. The sorbet is best served immediately or can be kept in the freezer for up to 3–4 days.

mixed berry sorbet
sorbetto ai frutti di bosco

In Italian, *frutti di bosco* is translated as 'fruits from the forest'. It is one of the most popular flavours and is fabulous in combination with the Sorrento Lemon Sorbet or Custard Cream Gelato.

360 ml/1½ cups spring water

freshly squeezed juice of ½ lemon

160 g/¾ cup plus 1 tablespoon organic (caster) sugar

500 g/1 lb. 2 oz. ripe organic berries, such as raspberries, wild strawberries (hulled), blackberries and blueberries

Serves 4

In a saucepan set over medium heat, gently heat 160 ml/⅔ cup of the spring water until it reaches boiling point. Remove from the heat, add the lemon juice and stir in the sugar until it dissolves. Let the syrup cool for 30 minutes.

Put the berries and the remaining water in a food processor and blitz to a purée. Add the cooled syrup and blend briefly again until thoroughly mixed.

Pour the mixture into the gelato maker and churn freeze according to the manufacturer's instructions.

The sorbet is best served immediately or can be kept in the freezer for up to 3–4 days.

pear sorbet

sorbetto alla pera

The Doyenne du Comice variety is the perfect dessert pear – sweet and juicy with a melting flesh, it makes a wonderfully scented sorbet. Teamed with the chocolate gelato it is almost unbeatable.

535 ml/2⅓ cups spring water

freshly squeezed juice of 1 lemon

160 g/¾ cup plus 1 tablespoon organic (caster) sugar

675 g/1 lb. 8 oz. ripe organic Comice pears (about 3 pears), peeled, cored and chopped

For the pear slices

1 ripe organic Comice pear

1 tablespoon (caster) sugar

a baking sheet lined with baking parchment

Serves 4

In a saucepan set over medium heat, gently heat 160 ml/⅔ cup of the spring water until it reaches boiling point. Remove from the heat, add half the lemon juice and stir in the sugar until it dissolves. Let the syrup cool for 30 minutes.

Put the pears and the remaining water in a food processor and blitz to a purée. Add the cooled syrup and the remaining lemon juice and blend briefly again until thoroughly mixed.

Pour the mixture into the gelato maker and churn freeze according to the manufacturer's instructions.

To make the pear slices, preheat the oven to 150°C (300°F) Gas 2.

Using a mandolin or a very sharp knife, thinly slice the pear. Place the slices on the prepared baking sheet and sprinkle over the sugar. Bake in the preheated oven for 20 minutes or until golden brown.

Serve the sorbet in bowls, garnished with a pear slice.

The sorbet is best served immediately or can be kept in the freezer for up to 3–4 days. Serve with a baked pear slice on the side.

green apple sorbet
sorbetto alla mela verde

Slightly tart apples, such as Granny Smiths, make a crisp, refreshing sorbet. Either peel the apples for a smoother texture or, as here, leave the skins on so pretty flecks of green are visible in the sorbet.

285 ml/1 cup plus 2 tablespoons spring water

freshly squeezed juice of 1 lemon

160 g/¾ cup plus 1 tablespoon organic (caster) sugar

675 g/1 lb. 8 oz. ripe organic Granny Smith apples (about 6 apples), cored and chopped

Serves 4

In a saucepan set over medium heat, gently heat 160 ml/⅔ cup of the spring water until it reaches boiling point. Remove from the heat, add half the lemon juice and stir in the sugar until it dissolves. Let the syrup cool for 30 minutes.

Put the apples and the remaining water in a food processor and blitz to a purée. Add the cooled syrup and the remaining lemon juice and blend briefly again until thoroughly mixed.

Pour the mixture into the gelato maker and churn freeze according to the manufacturer's instructions.

The sorbet is best served immediately or can be kept in the freezer for up to 3–4 days.

apricot sorbet
sorbetto all'albicocca

Ripe, juicy apricots make a fragrant summer sorbet. Apricots have long been considered an aphrodisiac and there is a no more potent way to serve them than in highly-pleasurable scoops of sorbet.

410 ml/1⅔ cups spring water
freshly squeezed juice of 1 lemon
160 g/¾ cup plus 1 tablespoon
   organic (caster) sugar
450 g/1 lb. ripe organic apricots
   (about 12–13 apricots), halved
   and pitted

Serves 4

In a saucepan set over medium heat, gently heat 160 ml/⅔ cup of the spring water until it reaches boiling point. Remove from the heat, add half the lemon juice and stir in the sugar until it dissolves. Let the syrup cool for 30 minutes.

Put the apricots and the remaining water in a food processor and blitz to a purée. Add the cooled syrup and the remaining lemon juice and blend briefly again until thoroughly mixed.

Pour the mixture into the gelato maker and churn freeze according to the manufacturer's instructions.

The sorbet is best served immediately or can be kept in the freezer for up to 3–4 days.

italian peach sorbet
sorbetto alla pesca italiana

Italian peaches are some of the best in the world, but you may have to take our word for it as soft fruits do not travel well over long distances. Wherever you are, it is always far better to use locally-grown, fresh, fuzzy peaches for the sweetest sorbet.

410 ml/1⅔ cups spring water

freshly squeezed juice of ½ lemon

210 g/1 cup organic (caster) sugar

400 g/14 oz. ripe organic peaches (about 3 peaches), halved and pitted

Serves 4

In a saucepan set over medium heat, gently heat 160 ml/⅔ cup of the spring water until it reaches boiling point. Remove from the heat, add half the lemon juice and stir in 150 g/¾ cup of the sugar until it dissolves. Let the syrup cool for 30 minutes.

Put the peaches and the remaining water and sugar in a food processor and blitz to a purée. Add the cooled syrup and the remaining lemon juice and blend briefly again until thoroughly mixed.

Pour the mixture into the gelato maker and churn freeze according to the manufacturer's instructions.

The sorbet is best served immediately or can be kept in the freezer for up to 3–4 days.

coconut sorbet
sorbetto al cocco

If you see fresh hairy-shelled coconuts on the market, a sorbet is a great way to enjoy them. Extracting the coconut flesh can sometimes be fiddly, but the result will be well worth the effort.

160 ml/⅔ cup spring water
freshly squeezed juice of ½ lemon
210 g/1 cup organic (caster) sugar
150 g/5 oz. fresh coconut, skin removed and chopped
500 ml/2 cups organic coconut milk

Serves 4

In a saucepan set over medium heat, gently heat the spring water until it reaches boiling point. Remove from the heat, add the lemon juice and stir in the sugar until it dissolves. Let the syrup cool for 30 minutes.

Put the coconut pieces and the coconut milk in a food processor and blitz until all the coconut pieces are puréed and the mixture is smooth. Add the cooled syrup and blend briefly again until thoroughly mixed.

Pour the mixture into the gelato maker and churn freeze according to the manufacturer's instructions.

The sorbet is best served immediately or can be kept in the freezer for up to 3–4 days.

sicilian blood orange sorbet
sorbetto all'arancia rossa siciliana

Sicily is well known for its blood oranges, so called because of their deep red juice and flesh. They are more tart than regular oranges, and result in a tangy and refreshing sorbet.

360 ml/1½ cups spring water
freshly squeezed juice of ½ lemon
210 g/1 cup organic (caster) sugar
400 ml/1⅔ cups freshly squeezed
   blood orange juice (about
   9 oranges)

Serves 4

In a saucepan set over medium heat, gently heat 160 ml/⅔ cup of the spring water until it reaches boiling point. Remove from the heat, add half the lemon juice and stir in 150 g/¾ cup of the sugar until it dissolves. Let the syrup cool for 30 minutes.

Put the orange juice and the remaining water and sugar in a jug/pitcher and whisk them together. Add the cooled syrup and whisk briefly again until thoroughly mixed.

Pour the mixture into the gelato maker and churn freeze according to the manufacturer's instructions.

The sorbet is best served immediately or can be kept in the freezer for up to 3–4 days.

mandarin sorbet
sorbetto al mandarino

Like the lemon sorbet, mandarin sorbet is a great palate cleanser and so is perfect for enjoying between courses at a celebration dinner. Among all the mandarin varieties, we suggest using clementines, although, as with all fruit, only use them when in season!

340 ml/1½ cups spring water
freshly squeezed juice of ½ lemon
180 g/¾ cup plus 2 tablespoons organic (caster) sugar
400 ml/1⅔ cups freshly squeezed organic mandarin juice

Serves 4

In a saucepan set over medium heat, gently heat 160 ml/⅔ cup of the spring water until it reaches boiling point. Remove from the heat, add the lemon juice and stir in all but 2 tablespoons of the sugar until it dissolves. Let the syrup cool for 30 minutes.

Put the mandarin juice and the remaining water and sugar in a jug/pitcher and whisk them together. Add the cooled syrup and whisk briefly again until thoroughly mixed.

Pour the mixture into the gelato maker and churn freeze according to the manufacturer's instructions.

The sorbet is best served immediately or can be kept in the freezer for up to 3–4 days.

alphonso mango sorbet
sorbetto al mango alfonso

When the Alphonso mango is in season, this sorbet is simply unmissable. Rich in flavour, colour and aroma, they are thought to be the best variety of mango and give this sorbet an indulgent edge.

410 ml/1⅔ cups spring water

freshly squeezed juice of ½ lemon

160 g/¾ cup plus 1 tablespoon organic (caster) sugar

450 g/1 lb. ripe organic Alphonso mangoes (about 2 mangoes), peeled, pitted and chopped

Serves 4

In a saucepan set over medium heat, gently heat 160 ml/⅔ cup of the spring water until it reaches boiling point. Remove from the heat, add the lemon juice and stir in the sugar until it dissolves. Let the syrup cool for 30 minutes.

Put the mango and the remaining water in a food processor and blitz to a purée. Add the cooled syrup and blend briefly again until thoroughly mixed.

Pour the mixture into the gelato maker and churn freeze according to the manufacturer's instructions.

The sorbet is best served immediately or can be kept in the freezer for up to 3–4 days.

dottato fig sorbet
sorbetto al fico dottato

Figs are native to the Mediterranean region and appear in many Italian dishes. The Dottato variety is prized in the south of Italy, but if you can't find them locally, use the best available in season.

410 ml/1⅔ cups spring water

freshly squeezed juice of ½ lemon

210 g/1 cup organic (caster) sugar

400 g/14 oz. ripe organic Dottato (Kadota) figs, stalks removed and halved

Serves 4

In a saucepan set over medium heat, gently heat 160 ml/⅔ cup of the spring water until it reaches boiling point. Remove from the heat, add the lemon juice and stir in 150 g/¾ cup of the sugar until it dissolves. Let the syrup cool for 30 minutes.

Put the figs in a food processor with the remaining water and sugar and blitz to a purée. Add the cooled syrup and blend briefly again until thoroughly mixed.

Pour the mixture into the gelato maker and churn freeze according to the manufacturer's instructions.

The sorbet is best served immediately or can be kept in the freezer for up to 3–4 days.

cantaloupe melon sorbet

sorbetto al melone cantaloupe

The cantaloupe melon has a special link with Italy, named as it is after the commune Cantolupo near Tivoli, where the Pope used to spend his summers. It is sweet and juicy and perfect for sorbets.

310 ml/1⅓ cups spring water

freshly squeezed juice of ½ lemon

210 g/1 cup organic (caster) sugar

400 g/14 oz. cantaloupe melon peeled, deseeded and chopped (about ½ melon)

Serves 4

In a saucepan set over medium heat, gently heat 160 ml/⅔ cup of the spring water until it reaches boiling point. Remove from the heat, add the lemon juice and stir in 150 g/¾ cup of the sugar until it dissolves. Let the syrup cool for 30 minutes.

Put the melon and the remaining water and sugar in a food processor and blitz to a purée. Add the cooled syrup and the remaining lemon juice and blend briefly again until thoroughly mixed.

Pour the mixture into the gelato maker and churn freeze according to the manufacturer's instructions.

The sorbet is best served immediately or can be kept in the freezer for up to 3–4 days.

cherry sorbet

sorbetto alla ciliegia

If this sweet sorbet is simply not enough cherry for you, try serving it with a cherry on top! Amarena cherries preserved in syrup are an Italian speciality and are the perfect accompaniment spooned over the sorbet.

410 ml/1⅔ cups spring water
freshly squeezed juice of 1 lemon
160 g/¾ cup plus 1 tablespoon
  organic (caster) sugar
450 g/1 lb. ripe organic cherries,
  pitted

Serves 4

In a saucepan set over medium heat, gently heat 160 ml/⅔ cup of the spring water until it reaches boiling point. Remove from the heat, add half the lemon juice and stir in the sugar until it dissolves. Let the syrup cool for 30 minutes.

Put the pitted cherries and the remaining water in a food processor and blitz to a purée. Add the cooled syrup and the remaining lemon juice and blend briefly again until thoroughly mixed.

Pour the mixture into the gelato maker and churn freeze according to the manufacturer's instructions.

The sorbet is best served immediately or can be kept in the freezer for up to 3–4 days.

kiwi fruit sorbet
sorbetto al kiwi

Like the fruit, our kiwi sorbet is delicately flavoured and so distinguishable by it's pretty pale green colour and little black seeds. Kiwi also has one of the highest levels of vitamin C of any fruit, so this sorbet is purely medicinal!

560 ml/2¼ cups spring water
freshly squeezed juice of ½ lemon
210 g/1 cup organic (caster) sugar
400 g/14 oz. ripe organic kiwi
**   fruit, peeled and chopped**

Serves 4

In a saucepan set over medium heat, gently heat 160 ml/⅔ cup of the spring water until it reaches boiling point. Remove from the heat, add the lemon juice and stir in 150 g/¾ cup of the sugar until it dissolves. Let the syrup cool for 30 minutes.

Put the kiwi fruit and the remaining water and sugar in a food processor and blitz to a purée. Add the cooled syrup and blend briefly again until thoroughly mixed.

Pour the mixture into the gelato maker and churn freeze according to the manufacturer's instructions.

The sorbet is best served immediately or can be kept in the freezer for up to 3–4 days.

raspberry sorbet
sorbetto al lampone

At Dri Dri we serve this flavour in the summer months when we are able to source high quality English raspberries from local growers. Our delicious recipe contains fifty per cent crushed fresh raspberries for a refreshing treat.

415 ml/1⅔ cups spring water
freshly squeezed juice of 1 lemon
240 g/1¼ cups organic (caster) sugar
450 g/1 lb. ripe organic raspberries

Serves 4

In a saucepan set over medium heat, gently heat 240 ml/1 cup of the spring water until it reaches boiling point. Remove from the heat, add half the lemon juice and stir in the sugar until it dissolves. Let the syrup cool for 30 minutes.

Put the raspberries and the remaining water in a food processor and blitz to a purée. Add the cooled syrup and the remaining lemon juice and blend briefly again until thoroughly mixed.

Pour the mixture into the gelato maker and churn freeze according to the manufacturer's instructions.

The sorbet is best served immediately or can be kept in the freezer for up to 3–4 days.

blackberry sorbet
sorbetto alla mora

Our blackberry sorbet is delicious either served alone or in perfect combination with the White Chocolate and Hazelnut or Custard Cream gelato. Just one word of warning: don't pick your autumn blackberries after Old Michelmas Day on 11th October, as folklore tells that the devil will have claimed them!

415 ml/1⅔ cups spring water

freshly squeezed juice of ½ lemon

240 g/1¼ cups organic (caster) sugar

400 g/14 oz. ripe organic blackberries

Serves 4

In a saucepan set over medium heat, gently heat 160 ml/⅔ cup of the spring water until it reaches boiling point. Remove from the heat, add the lemon juice and stir in the sugar until it dissolves. Let the syrup cool for 30 minutes.

Put the blackberries and the remaining water in a food processor and blitz to a purée. Add the cooled syrup and blend briefly again until thoroughly mixed.

Pour the mixture into the gelato maker and churn freeze according to the manufacturer's instructions.

The sorbet is best served immediately or can be kept in the freezer for up to 3–4 days.

Granita

coffee granita
granita al caffé

Coffee is one of the most traditional flavours of granita. It is served all over Italy, often with a drizzle of cream. As with the coffee gelato, always ensure that you are using the best quality arabica coffee you can find.

450 ml/1¾ cups spring water

180 g/¾ cup plus 2 tablespoons organic (caster) sugar

300 ml/1¼ cups espresso made with organic 100% Arabica coffee beans, cooled

chocolate-coated coffee beans, to serve (optional)

Serves 4

In a saucepan set over medium heat, gently heat the spring water until it reaches boiling point. Remove from the heat and stir in the sugar until it dissolves. Let the syrup cool for 30 minutes.

When the syrup has cooled, add the espresso and stir together.

Pour the mixture into the gelato maker and churn freeze according to the manufacturer's instructions.

When it is ready, transfer the mixture to a shallow container. Return to the freezer for 1 hour to firm up. Remove from the freezer and use a fork to scrape the surface of the ice to produce coarse granules. You can also do this straight from the gelato maker for a softer finish.

Spoon the granules into glasses or bowl and serve immediately with chocolate-coated coffee beans, if using.

english strawberry granita
granita alla fragola inglese

Although granita hails from Siciliy, and was thought to have originally been made from snow collected from the slopes of Mount Etna, the quintessential English strawberry lends itself very well as a flavouring.

750 ml/3 cups spring water
freshly squeezed juice of 1 lemon
200 g/1 cup organic (caster) sugar
500 g/1 lb. 2 oz. ripe organic
strawberries, hulled

Serves 4

In a saucepan set over medium heat, gently heat the spring water until it reaches boiling point. Remove from the heat, add the lemon juice and stir in the sugar until it dissolves. Let the syrup cool for 30 minutes.

Put the strawberries in a food processor and blitz to a purée. Add the cooled syrup and blend briefly again until thoroughly mixed.

Pour the mixture into the gelato maker and churn freeze according to the manufacturer's instructions.

When it is ready, transfer the mixture to a shallow container. Return to the freezer for 1 hour to firm up. Remove from the freezer and use a fork to scrape the surface of the ice to produce coarse granules. You can also do this straight from the gelato maker for a softer finish.

Spoon the granules into glasses or bowls and serve immediately.

french cherry granita
granita alla ciliegia francese

The simplicity of granita is the perfect way to appreciate the season's pick of cherries. With nothing added but pure water and a hint of sweetness, their flavour shines through.

300 ml/1¼ cups spring water
freshly squeezed juice of 1 lemon
100 g/½ cup organic (caster) sugar
400 g/14 oz. ripe organic cherries, pitted

Serves 4

In a saucepan set over medium heat, gently heat the spring water until it reaches boiling point. Remove from the heat, add the lemon juice and stir in the sugar until it dissolves. Let the syrup cool for 30 minutes.

Put the cherries in a food processor and blitz to a purée. Add the cooled syrup and blend briefly again until thoroughly mixed.

Pour the mixture into the gelato maker and churn freeze according to the manufacturer's instructions.

When it is ready, transfer the mixture to a shallow container. Return to the freezer for 1 hour to firm up. Remove from the freezer and use a fork to scrape the surface of the ice to produce coarse granules. You can also do this straight from the gelato maker for a softer finish.

Spoon the granules into glasses or bowls and serve immediately.

sorrento lemon granita
granita al limone di sorrento

In Italy, it is popular to serve lemon granita for breakfast. The tangy citrussy flavour is a refreshing way to wake up on a balmy Italian morning. Enjoy alone or served with the brioche on page 110.

750 ml/3 cups spring water

250 g/1¼ cups organic (caster) sugar

180 ml/¾ cup freshly squeezed organic lemon juice (about 5 lemons)

Serves 4

In a saucepan set over medium heat, gently heat the spring water until it reaches boiling point. Remove from the heat and stir in the sugar until it dissolves. Let the syrup cool for 30 minutes.

When the syrup has cooled, add the lemon juice and stir briefly to mix. Pour into the gelato maker and churn freeze according to the manufacturer's instructions.

When it is ready, transfer the mixture to a shallow container. Return to the freezer for 1 hour to firm up. Remove from the freezer and use a fork to scrape the surface of the ice to produce coarse granules. You can also do this straight from the gelato maker for a softer finish.

Spoon the granules into glasses or bowls and serve immediately.

blood orange granita
granita all'arancia rossa

Blood oranges, so called because of the deep red colour of their flesh and juice, are particularly associated with Sicily and add authenticity to this classic Sicilian dessert.

400 ml/1¾ cups spring water
200 g/1 cup organic (caster) sugar
600 ml/2½ cups freshly squeezed organic blood orange juice (about 15 oranges)

Serves 4

In a saucepan set over medium heat, gently heat the spring water until it reaches boiling point. Remove from the heat and stir in the sugar until it dissolves. Let the syrup cool for 30 minutes.

Pass the blood orange juice through a sieve/strainer to remove any pips or bits of flesh.

When the syrup has cooled, add the blood orange juice and stir briefly to mix. Pour into the gelato maker and churn freeze according to the manufacturer's instructions.

When it is ready, transfer the mixture to a shallow container. Return to the freezer for 1 hour to firm up. Remove from the freezer and use a fork to scrape the surface of the ice to produce coarse granules. You can also do this straight from the gelato maker for a softer finish.

Spoon the granules into glasses or bowls and serve immediately.

chocolate granita
granita al cioccolato

Without dairy to soften and temper the taste of the chocolate, the flavour of this granita is deep and sophisticated and definitely one for real chocolate afficionados. Try to use cocoa marked as 'gran cru' or even 'premier cru' chocolate – which means the cocoa beans all come from the same country or, even better, the same region – as it is a guarantee of good quality.

1 litre/4¼ cups spring water
300 g/1½ cups organic (caster) sugar
120 g/1 scant cup unsweetened cocoa powder

Serves 4

In a saucepan set over medium heat, gently heat the spring water until it reaches boiling point. Remove from the heat and stir in the sugar and cocoa powder until it dissolves. Set the syrup aside to cool for 30 minutes.

When cooled, pour the chocolate syrup into the gelato maker and churn freeze according to the manufacturer's instructions.

When it is ready, transfer the mixture to a shallow container. Return to the freezer for 1 hour to firm up. Remove from the freezer and use a fork to scrape the surface of the ice to produce coarse granules. You can also do this straight from the gelato maker for a softer finish.

Spoon the granules into glasses or bowls and serve immediately.

Serving gelato

gelato sandwich with florentines

Florentines make a perfect partner for a scoop of luxurious gelato, and make an indulgent afternoon treat. The florentines are easy to prepare and can be used to make a sandwich of whichever gelato flavour is your favourite.

50 g/3 tablespoons organic butter

50 g/¼ cup organic (caster) sugar

3 tablespoons double/heavy cream

25 g/3 tablespoons flaked/slivered almonds

75 g/½ cup mixed nuts, such as hazelnuts, walnuts and pistachios, finely chopped

4 glacé/candied cherries, finely chopped

50 g/¼ cup mixed glacé/candied fruits, such as citrus peel, apricots, pineapple and angelica, finely chopped

25 g/3 tablespoons plain/all-purpose flour

4 scoops of gelato in your favourite flavour

2 baking sheets, lined with baking parchment and well greased

Makes 4 sandwiches

Preheat the oven to 180°C (350°F) Gas 4.

Very gently heat the butter, sugar and cream in a small saucepan, stirring, until melted. Bring to the boil, then remove from the heat and stir in the nuts, glacé fruits and flour until thoroughly mixed.

Drop tablespoonfuls of the mixture onto the prepared baking sheets to create 8 mounds, spaced well apart. Bake in the preheated oven for about 10 minutes until golden. Remove from the oven and gently press back the edges using a palette knife to make neat rounds. Let cool on the baking sheets for about 10 minutes until firm, then carefully peel off the baking parchment and, using a spatula, transfer to a wire rack to cool completely.

To assemble the sandwiches, place a florentine on a plate, top with a scoop of freshly made gelato and finish with another florentine on top. Assemble 4 florentine sandwiches in this way and serve immediately before the gelato melts.

hot chocolate brownie with gelato

Hot chocolate brownie with gelato melting over the top is unadulterated indulgence. These dense, gooey brownies are quick and simple to make, and pair perfectly with the richer gelatos such as White Chocolate and Hazelnut, Espresso or Madagascan Vanilla.

225 g/8 oz. dark chocolate (70% cocoa solids), chopped

150 g/10 tablespoons organic butter, diced

125 g/½ cup organic (caster) sugar

125 g/½ cup plus 1 tablespoon light muscovado/light brown sugar

4 free-range eggs, lightly beaten

1 teaspoon vanilla extract

125 g/1 cup plain/all-purpose flour

a pinch of salt

scoops of gelato in your favourite flavour, to serve

a 23-cm/9-inch square baking pan, greased and lined with greased baking parchment

Makes 16 squares

Preheat the oven to 170°C (325°F) Gas 3.

Put the chocolate and butter in a heatproof bowl set over a saucepan of barely simmering water. Stir until smooth and thoroughly combined. Leave to cool slightly.

Add both the sugars and mix well. Add the eggs one at a time, beating well after each addition. Stir in the vanilla extract. Sift the flour and salt into the bowl and stir until smooth.

Pour the mixture into the prepared baking pan, spread level with a spatula and bake on the middle shelf of the preheated oven for about 20–25 minutes, or until the brownies are set and have a light crust on top.

Remove from the oven and leave to cool a little before cutting into squares. Serve the warm squares topped with a scoop of gelato in your chosen flavour.

sicilian brioche with lemon sorbet

In Sicily, it is traditional to serve lemon sorbet or granita in a brioche for breakfast. If you want warm brioches for breakfast, you can make and shape the dough the night before, ready for baking in the morning.

500 g/4 cups strong white bread flour

7 g/¼ oz. easy-blend/active dried yeast

1 teaspoon sea salt

175 g/1½ sticks organic unsalted butter, diced

50 g/¼ cup organic (caster) sugar

3 large free-range eggs, at room temperature

150 ml/⅔ cup organic whole milk, lukewarm

1 free-range egg, beaten, to glaze

1 quantity of Sorrento Lemon Sorbet (page 56) or Granita (page 98)

a 12-hole muffin pan or 12 mini fluted baking pans, well-greased

Makes 12 brioche

Put the flour, yeast and salt in the bowl of a large electric stand mixer and mix by hand. Add the butter and rub into the flour with your fingertips until the mixture looks like fine crumbs. Mix in the sugar. Beat the eggs with the milk until thoroughly combined, then add to the flour mixture. Using the dough hook attachment of the mixer, mix the ingredients on low speed until you get a heavy, sticky dough. Scrape down the sides, then knead the dough in the machine on low speed for 5 minutes until glossy, very smooth and soft. Alternatively, if you don't have a food mixer, mix the ingredients as above, then knead the dough by hand. Cover and leave to rise at normal room temperature (not too warm) until doubled in size, 1½–2 hours.

Turn out the risen dough onto a lightly floured work surface. Punch down, then knead gently for about 1 minute. Divide the dough into 12 equal portions and roll into smooth, neat balls. Drop into the muffin pan. Slip the pan into a large plastic bag, slightly inflate, then leave to rise until doubled in size, about 1 hour in a warm kitchen or overnight in the fridge.

When ready to continue, preheat the oven to 200°C (400°F) Gas 6.

Uncover the brioches and lightly brush with beaten egg to glaze. Bake in the preheated oven for 18–20 minutes until firm and a good golden colour. Leave to cool for a minute for the crust to firm up then carefully turn out onto a wire rack to cool completely.

When ready to serve, slice the brioche in half with a serrated knife and fill with lemon granita. Or, if preferred, simply serve the brioche on the side of a bowl of granita.

custard cream, raspberry and chocolate gelato cake

Gelato and sorbet are perfect for combining and creating new flavours. For a special occasion, layer them up over an amaretti biscuit base to make this spectacular frozen cake. The flavours here are suggestions, so do feel free to experiment with your favourites!

400 g/14 oz. amaretti
biscuits/cookies

90 g/6 tablespoons organic
unsalted butter, melted

1 quantity of Chocolate Gelato
(page 18)

1 quantity of Raspberry Sorbet
(page 86)

1 quantity of Custard Cream
Gelato (page 47)

a 20 x 30-cm/8 x 12-inch baking
pan, lined with baking
parchment

Serves 8

To make the biscuit base for the cake, crush the amaretti biscuits/ cookies untill you get fine crumbs. You can use a food processor or put them in a plastic bag and pound with a rolling pin. Put the crumbs into a large mixing bowl and pour in the melted butter. Stir thoroughly so all the crumbs are coated in the butter and then tip them into the prepared baking pan. Use the back of a spoon to level the crumbs, pressing them down into the pan. Put the pan in the refrigerator to chill and set the base while you make the gelato.

Begin to prepare your three flavours of gelato and sorbet one at a time, starting with chocolate, as this will be added to the pan first. When the Chocolate Gelato is ready, pour it directly from the gelato maker and into the pan. Put the pan in the freezer to keep cool while you make the Raspberry Sorbet. Layer the sorbet in the same way and freeze again while you prepare the Custard Cream Gelato. When all 3 flavours are layered in the pan, chill in the freezer for a few hours or overnight so it can firm up.

When you are ready to serve the cake, turn it out onto a plate and remove the baking parchment. Invert your serving plate and place it on top of the gelato cake. Turn both plates simultaneously so the gelato cake sits base-down on the serving plate. Cut into slices and serve immediately.

almond affogato

gelato alla mandorla affogato al caffe'

Affogato, meaning 'drowned', is a classic Italian way to serve gelato. Drown scoops of gelato with a shot of hot espresso. Almond and coffee is a perfect combination, but you could try it with other gelato flavours such as Madagascan Vanilla, Bacio or Hazelnut. This recipe makes enough gelato for eight servings, but if fewer servings are required, simply store the remaining gelato in the freezer to enjoy another time.

500 ml/2 cups organic whole milk

165 ml/⅔ cup organic whipping cream

140 g/1 cup shelled almonds

½ teaspoon of sea salt

165 g/¾ cup organic (caster) sugar

1 free-range egg white

shots espresso made with organic 100% Arabica beans, to serve

Serves 8

Put the milk and cream in a small saucepan and heat gently until it reaches boiling point. Pour the mixture into a heat-resistant bowl and refrigerate for 20 minutes.

In a dry frying pan/skillet, lightly toast the almonds with the salt and set aside to cool. When cooled, grind the almonds to a paste in a food processor.

In a large mixing bowl and using an electric hand whisk, beat together the sugar and egg white until it forms soft peaks when the beaters are lifted out of the mixture. Stir in the almond paste, add the chilled milk mixture and whisk for a further 20 seconds.

Pour the mixture into the gelato maker and churn freeze according to the manufacturer's instructions.

Prepare shots of espresso using an espresso machine or an Italian moka. Place a scoop of the gelato into each coffee cup and serve with a shot of espresso on the side so guests can pour the hot coffee over the gelato and enjoy immediately.

rossini

The Rossini is a variation of the classic Bellini, with strawberries replacing the fresh peaches. It was named after the Italian composer Gioachino Rossini.

1 quantity English Strawberry
    Sorbet (page 51), prepared
    following the method below
300 ml/1¼ cups Franciacorta
    Prosecco wine

Serves 8

Prepare the sorbet as directed in the method on page 51. When the sorbet has finished churning, pour the Prosecco into the gelato maker and run the machine for a further 10 seconds to mix.

Pour into 8 small glasses and serve.

sgroppino

The Sgroppino originated in Venice in the 16th century, where aristocrats used the cocktail as a palate cleanser between courses. Now it is generally served after the meal, as a dessert or in addition to one. A simple lemon sorbet is mixed with sparkling Prosecco with wonderfully refreshing results.

600 ml/2½ cups spring water
200 g/1 cup organic (caster) sugar
200 ml/¾ cup freshly squeezed
    organic lemon juice (about
    5 lemons)
100 ml/⅓ cup plus 1 tablespoon
    vodka
200 ml/¾ cup Franciacorta
    Prosecco wine
lemon slices, to garnish
fresh mint leaves, to garnish

Serves 4

In a saucepan set over medium heat, gently heat 160 ml/⅔ cup of the spring water until it reaches boiling point. Remove from the heat, add the sugar and stir until it dissolves. Let the syrup cool for 30 minutes.

When the syrup has cooled, add the lemon juice and the remaining spring water to the pan and whisk together to thoroughly mix.

Pour the mixture into the gelato maker and churn freeze according to the manufacturer's instructions.

When the sorbet has finished churning, pour the vodka and the Prosecco into the gelato maker and run the machine for a further 10 seconds to mix.

Spoon the sgroppino into 4 elegant, stemmed glasses, decorate each glass with a lemon slice and a mint leaf, and serve immediately.

margarita

Margaritas should always be served ice cold, so using a sorbet base is the perfect way to ensure this. For an authentic finish you could even frost the rim of the glass with salt before serving.

610 ml/2½ cups spring water
200 ml/¾ cup freshly squeezed organic lime juice (about 7 limes), 1 husk reserved
240 g/1 cup plus 3 tablespoons organic (caster) sugar
½ teaspooon sea salt, plus extra to frost the glass rim
300 ml/1¼ cups tequila
pared lime peel, to decorate

Serves 4

In a saucepan set over medium heat, gently heat 160 ml/⅔ cup of the water until it reaches boiling point. Remove from the heat, add 2 tablespoons of the lime juice and stir in 150 g/¾ cup of the sugar until it dissolves. Let the syrup cool for 30 minutes.

Put the remaining lime juice, water and sugar in a jug/pitcher and whisk together. Add the cooled syrup and whisk briefly again until thoroughly mixed.

Pour the mixture into the gelato maker and churn freeze according to the manufacturer's instructions.

While the sorbet is churning, prepare the glasses. Tip some sea salt onto a plate. Take the spent lime husk and run it around the top of a glass. Invert the glass and press it into the plate of salt to coat the rim.

When the sorbet has finished churning, pour the tequila and salt into the gelato maker and run the machine for a further 10 seconds to mix.

Spoon the margarita into the prepared glasses, decorate with pared lime peel and serve immediately.

mojito

This is a welcome twist to the classic Cuban Mojito. The job of 'muddling' the ice, citrus and mint is fulfilled by the gelato maker as it churns.

1 quantity Sorrento Lemon Sorbet (page 56), prepared following the method below
200 ml/¾ cup white rum
10 fresh mint leaves
4 lime wedges, to garnish

Serves 4

Prepare the sorbet as directed in the method on page 56. When the sorbet has finished churning, pour the rum into the gelato maker, add the mint leaves and run the machine for a further 10 seconds to mix.

Pour into glasses, garnish each glass with a lime wedge and serve immediately.

bellini

The Bellini is one of Italy's most loved cocktails. Use a variety of white peach and refreshing Italian Prosecco.

1 quantity Italian Peach Sorbet
300 ml/1¼ cups Franciacorta Prosecco wine

Serves 4

Place scoops of the peach sorbet into four glasses and pour the Prosecco over the sorbet, dividing it equally between the glasses, and serve immediately.

pina colada

Dream of lazy Caribbean days sipping this classic combination of pineapple, coconut and rum. Serve in hurricane glasses and add a little frivolity with a cocktail umbrella to evoke a real holiday spirit at home.

1 quantity Pineapple Sorbet (page 52), prepared following the method below

200 ml/¾ cup white rum

50 ml/¼ cup organic coconut milk

4 ripe organic pineapple wedges, to garnish

Serves 4

Prepare the sorbet as directed in the method on page 52. When the sorbet has finished churning, pour the rum and coconut milk into the gelato maker and run the machine for a further 10 seconds to mix.

Pour into hurricane glasses, garnish each glass with a pineapple wedge and serve immediately.

wild berries and crema milkshake
frullato di fragoline di bosco e crema

Wild strawberries have a stronger taste than cultivated varieties, and a much smaller berry. If you are lucky enough to find both these and a wild strawberry preserve, you will have something extraordinary, but made with regular strawberries it is perfectly delicious too!

1 quantity Custard Cream Gelato (page 47)

200 g/7 oz. ripe organic wild strawberries, hulled

200 ml/¾ cup organic whole milk, chilled

150 g/⅔ cup wild strawberry preserve, to serve (optional)

Serves 4

Put the Custard Cream Gelato, wild strawberries and milk into a blender and blitz until smooth.

Pour the shake into highball glasses, spoon a teaspoon of wild strawberry preserve into the drink and serve immediately with a straw.

flavour combinations

Gelato and sorbet flavour combinations are limited only by your imagination!
For an inspiration kick-start, here are some of the most requested flavour
pairings served in our shops, but you could always add a third flavour, too.

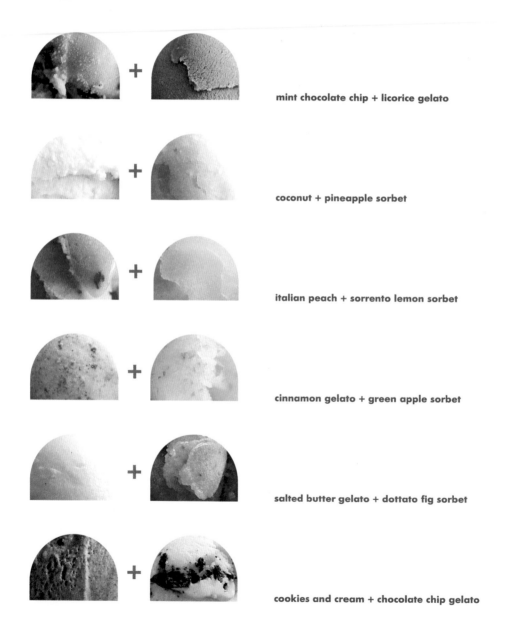

mint chocolate chip + licorice gelato

coconut + pineapple sorbet

italian peach + sorrento lemon sorbet

cinnamon gelato + green apple sorbet

salted butter gelato + dottato fig sorbet

cookies and cream + chocolate chip gelato

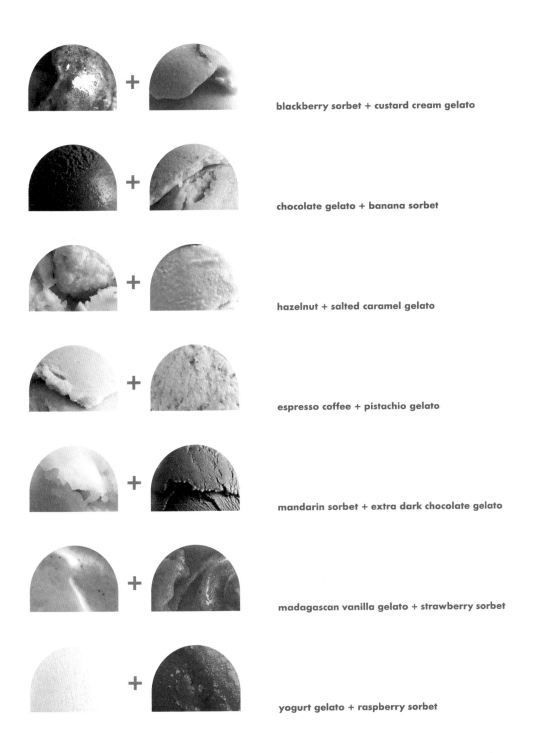

blackberry sorbet + custard cream gelato

chocolate gelato + banana sorbet

hazelnut + salted caramel gelato

espresso coffee + pistachio gelato

mandarin sorbet + extra dark chocolate gelato

madagascan vanilla gelato + strawberry sorbet

yogurt gelato + raspberry sorbet

Index